Recorder from the Beginning Tune Book 2

Twenty-three Solos and Twelve Duets to Complement
Recorder from the Beginning Book 2

John Pitts

Introduction

Recorder from the Beginning Tune Books 1, 2 and 3 provide material
to supplement the author's teaching scheme *Recorder from the
Beginning* Books 1, 2 and 3. This teaching scheme assumes no
previous knowledge of either music or the recorder and provides full
explanations at every stage. However, some children need more
practice material than others to consolidate their skills at particular
stages. Conversely, some pupils learn quickly and need extra
material to hold their interest while the rest of the group catch up.
The Tune Books provide for either situation, depending on individ-
ual needs.

All the material is carefully graded, following the order of pro-
gression in the teaching scheme. However, in keeping with the
"repertoire" nature of these supplementary books, very little teaching help or explanation is given. Where such help is required it is
best to refer to the appropriate pages of the teaching scheme. Cross-
references are provided for this purpose.

Acknowledgements

The publishers would like to thank Roberton Publications for permission to include
"Poor Fly" by Carey Blyton.

The music on page 14 and at the foot of page 21 has been specially arranged by the
author.

3-95

Contents

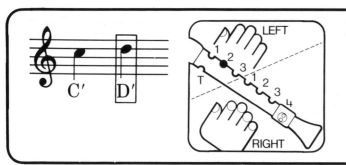

Extra tunes to try when you have played pages 2–5 in *Recorder from the Beginning 2.*

All Night, All Day (Spiritual)

All night, all ____ day, An——gels watching o-ver me, my Lord. ____

All night, all ____ day, An——gels watching o-ver me.

Now I lay me down to sleep, An——gels watching o-ver me, my Lord. ____

Pray the Lord my soul to keep, An——gels watching o-ver me.

Now I lay me

all ____ day,

me, my Lord. ____

Ask some friends to add an accompaniment to **All Night, All Day**.
They can use the three ostinati at the bottom of page 4.
Each pattern may be played either by itself or with the others.
If possible, use a different instrument for each ostinato:
for example, a xylophone, metallophone and glockenspiel.

When the Saints Go Marching In

Oh when the Saints _____ go mar–ching in, _____ Oh when the

Saints go mar——ching in, _____ I want to be a-

mong their num-ber, Oh when the Saints go mar——ching in.

One Man Went to Mow

More tunes using upper D (D')

Nobody Knows the Trouble I've Seen This piece has a two-part verse.

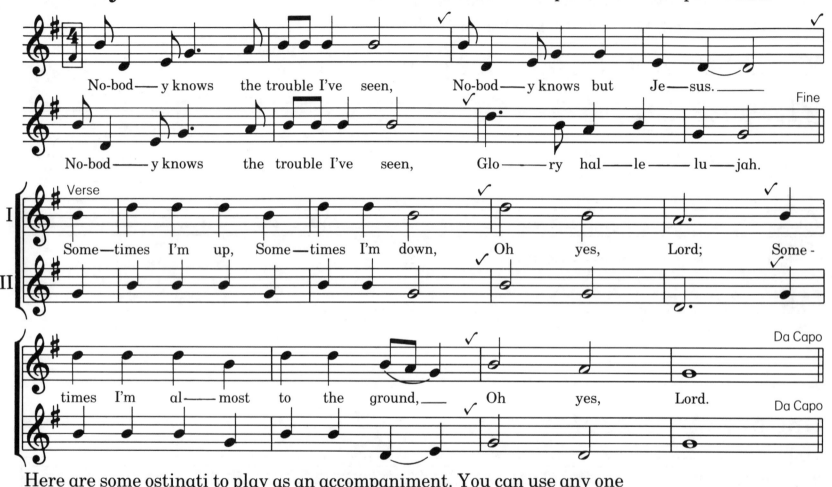

No-bod——y knows the trouble I've seen, No-bod——y knows but Je—sus._____

Fine

No-bod——y knows the trouble I've seen, Glo——ry hal—le——lu—jah.

I / **II**

Verse

Some—times I'm up, Some—times I'm down, Oh yes, Lord; Some -

times I'm al——most to the ground,___ Oh yes, Lord.

Da Capo

Da Capo

Here are some ostinati to play as an accompaniment. You can use any one
by itself or all three together. Choose a different instrument for each one.

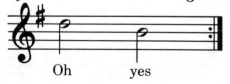

Oh yes

No-bod—y knows but

trouble I've seen,

Red River Valley (American)   Count 1–2–3 then play on count 4.

For a long time ___ now I've been wait — ing ___ for those
So then lin ——— ger a —while ere you leave us, ___ do not

words that you nev —— er will say.   And it's now that my fond heart is
ha —— sten to bid us a —dieu.   But re-mem —— ber the Red Riv — er

break -ing ___ for they say you are go ——— ing a — way. ___
Val —ley ___ and the mai ——— den who loved you so true. ___

Four in a Boat (American)

Four in a boat and the tide rolls high,   Four in a boat and the tide rolls high,

Four in a boat and the tide rolls high,   Wait-ing for a pret-ty one to come on by.

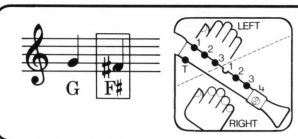

New note: F sharp (F♯)
See *Recorder from the Beginning 2*, pages 6–13.

Bella Bimba Count 1–2 then play on count 3.

Ma   co-me bal-li, bel-la bim—ba, bel-la bim—ba, bel-la bim—ba. Ma   ben!

Guar—da   che   pas—sa   la   vi—la—nel—la.   La é tan—to

bel——la   da_in-na—mo——rar'   Ah! _____   Ah! _____   Ah! ____

____   Ah! ___   Ma   co-me bal-li, bel-la   bim—ba,   bel-la   bim—ba,   bal-li   ben!

Add a rhythm accompaniment on claves and maracas, for example. Join in after the recorders have played their first note.

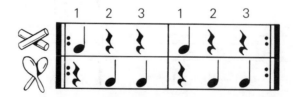

8

Cwm Rhondda (Welsh)

*Optional second part. The notes of the *tune* have stems pointing *up*: ♩ .
The notes of the *accompaniment* have stems pointing *down*: ♩ .

All through the Night (Welsh)

Ode to Joy (by Beethoven)   Take care with the tied note at the end of line 3.

Do Di Li (Israeli)

Fine

(clap   clap)   (clap   clap)

Da Capo

Oh Waly Waly (English)   Count 1–2–3–4–1 then play on count 2.

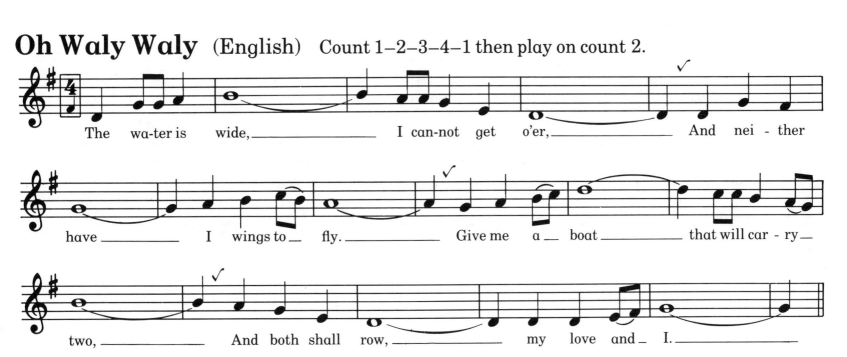

The   wa-ter is   wide,_____ I can-not get   o'er,_____ And   nei - ther

have _____ I wings to __ fly. _____ Give me   a __ boat _____ that will car - ry __

two, _____ And both shall   row, _____ my   love and _ I. _____

Ask a friend to accompany you on a triangle. Notice that the
recorder plays four notes before the triangle begins.

1–2 3–4   1–2 (3 4)

11

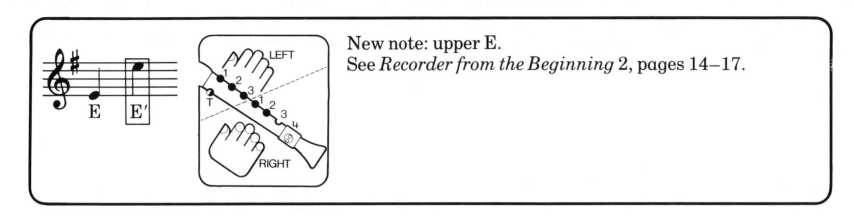

New note: upper E.
See *Recorder from the Beginning* 2, pages 14–17.

Turn the Glasses Over

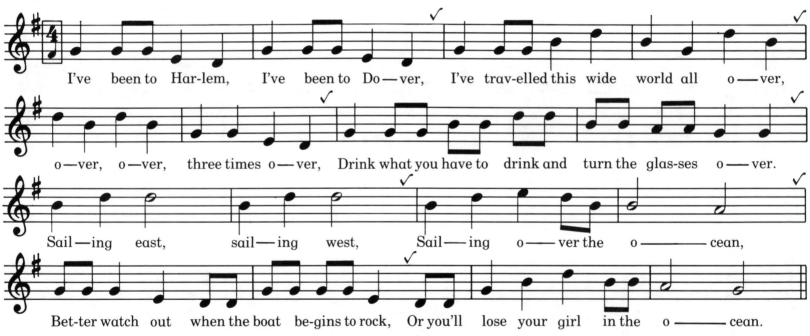

I've been to Har-lem, I've been to Do—ver, I've trav-elled this wide world all o—ver,

o—ver, o—ver, three times o—ver, Drink what you have to drink and turn the glas-ses o—ver.

Sail—ing east, sail—ing west, Sail—ing o—ver the o———cean,

Bet-ter watch out when the boat be-gins to rock, Or you'll lose your girl in the o———cean.

Ask some friends to add an accompaniment to **Turn the Glasses Over**. They can play any one or all three of the ostinato patterns opposite. It is best to use three different instruments: for example, a bass xylophone, metallophone and glockenspiel.

Everyone plays their pattern twice as an introduction before the recorders join in.
They then keep repeating the pattern all through the piece.

three times o——ver,

Drink what you have to drink

Sail——ing east,

Poor Fly (by Carey Blyton)

Two-part canon

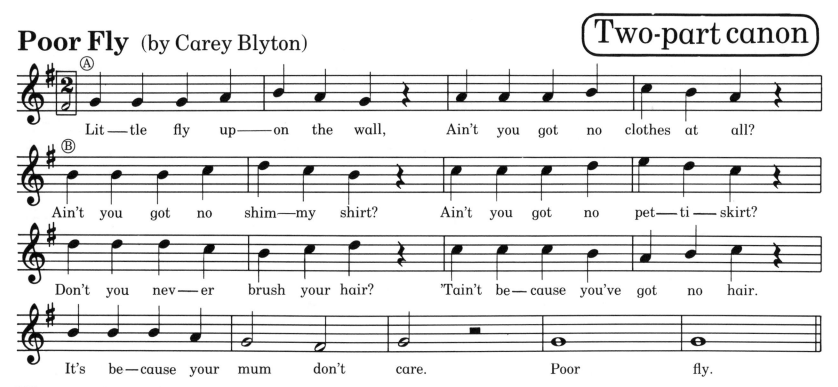

Lit—tle fly up——on the wall, Ain't you got no clothes at all?

Ain't you got no shim—my shirt? Ain't you got no pet—ti—skirt?

Don't you nev—er brush your hair? 'Tain't be—cause you've got no hair.

It's be—cause your mum don't care. Poor fly.

When you know this tune well, play it as a **canon** with your friends.
Divide into two groups. Group 1 starts. When they reach Ⓑ on the music,
Group 2 begins playing from Ⓐ. Later you can ask some singers to be
Group 1, with recorders as Group 2.

Mary Was Watching Tenderly (Czech)

Recorder I has the tune.

Arr. JCP

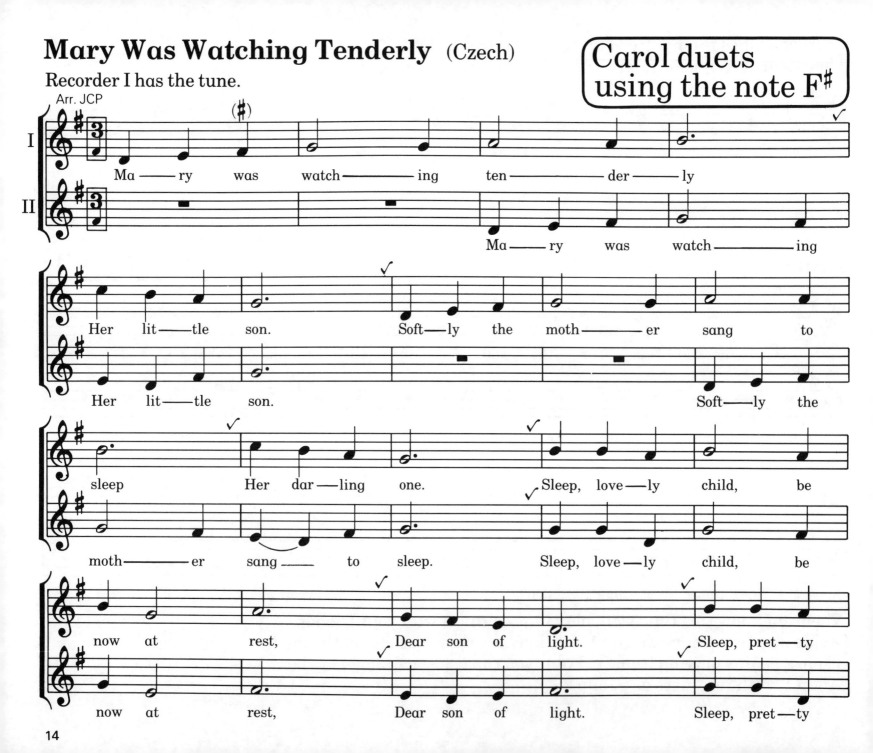

I — Ma — ry was watch — ing ten — der — ly

II — Ma — ry was watch — ing

Her lit — tle son. Soft — ly the moth — er sang to

Her lit — tle son. Soft — ly the

sleep Her dar — ling one. Sleep, love — ly child, be

moth — er sang to sleep. Sleep, love — ly child, be

now at rest, Dear son of light. Sleep, pret — ty

now at rest, Dear son of light. Sleep, pret — ty

14

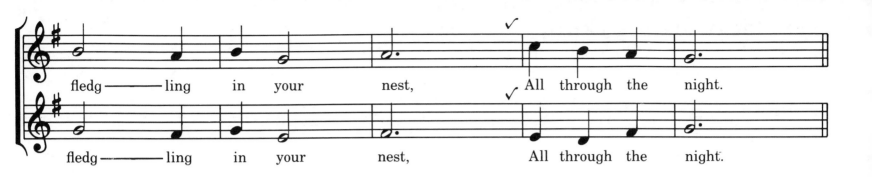

fledg —— ling in your nest, All through the night.

fledg —— ling in your nest, All through the night.

Under Bethlehem's Star so Bright (or Hydom, Hydom, Tydlidom) (Czech)

Ask two friends to accompany your duet.
They can use these ostinati all through the tune:

Both carol settings on pages 14 and 15 can be used with the music in *Carol, Gaily Carol*, published by A. & C. Black.

Sleigh-bells

Metallophone or
Xylophone or
Glockenspiel

Tyrolean Cradle Song (Austrian)

Recorder I counts 1–2 then plays on count 3.
A singer may take part I with a recorder playing part II.

Uses the note F#.

16

A Glad Nowell (or The Angels and the Shepherds) (Bohemian)

Uses the note E'.

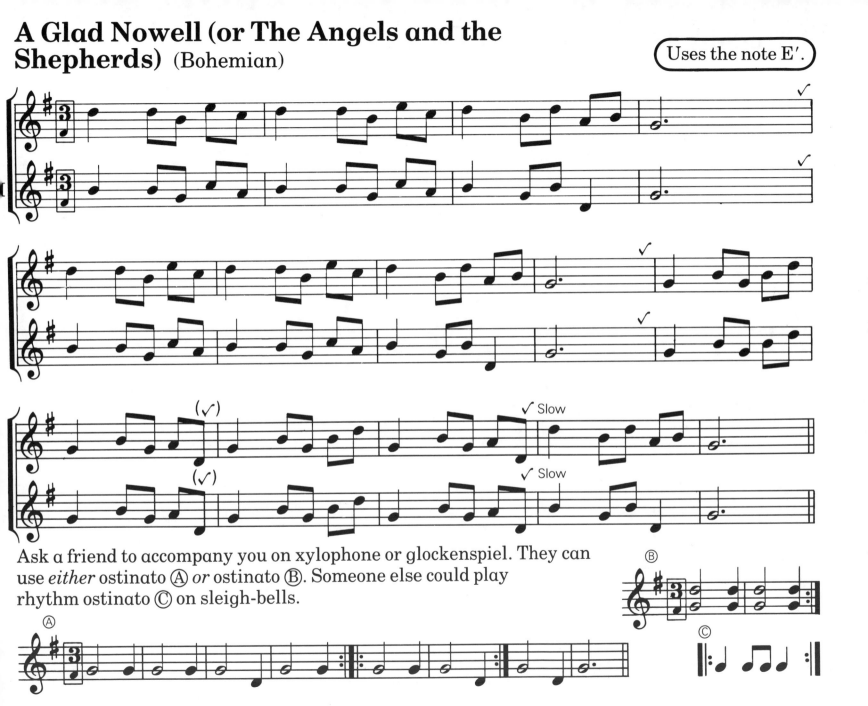

Ask a friend to accompany you on xylophone or glockenspiel. They can use *either* ostinato Ⓐ *or* ostinato Ⓑ. Someone else could play rhythm ostinato Ⓒ on sleigh-bells.

17

Three duets using upper E (E′)

Air (by Chédeville)   Play this fairly quickly. Count 1–2 then play on count 3.
Recorder I has the tune.

18

March (by Chédeville)

Rigaudon (by Chédeville) Count 1–2–3 then play on count 4.

20

Jingle Bells
(by J. Pierpoint)

New rhythms: ♫ ♩. ♫ ♫♫
See *Recorder from the Beginning* 2, pages 18–21.

Jin-gle bells! Jin-gle bells! Jin-gle all the way! Oh what fun it

is to ride in a one-horse o——pen sleigh. Oh, Jin-gle bells! Jin-gle bells!

Jin-gle all the way! Oh what fun it is to ride in a one-horse o——pen sleigh!

Cradle Song (by Schubert)   Play this duet slowly.

Arr. JCP

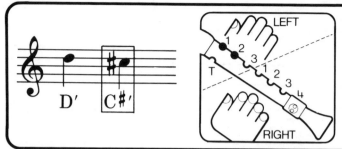

New note: C sharp (C#')
See *Recorder from the Beginning* 2, pages 24–27.

The Helston Furry Dance

Ask a friend to accompany **The Helston Furry Dance**.
They can use this rhythm on tambourine or drum:

Can-can

Add a tambourine accompaniment:

Menuetto (by Mozart)

Duet

23

Tinga Layo (West Indian)   Count 1–2–3 then play on count 4.   Duet

Ask some friends to play an accompaniment to **Tinga Layo** on maracas. They can use the word pattern "Come, little donkey" to help them keep to the rhythm.

Come, lit - tle don-key,

Later someone else can add claves (or a wooden block). Use the words "talk, my donkey" from the song to help keep to the rhythm.

talk, my don-key,

The percussion players begin after the recorders have played their first two notes.

Recorders

Tin-ga Lay———————o!

Percussion

1   2   3   4

Come, little donkey, Come, little donkey,

talk, my don-key,   talk, my don-key,

For a piano accompaniment to **Tinga Layo**, see *Class Music from the Beginning. Second Teacher's Book*, by Jan Holdstock and John Pitts, published by Arnold-Wheaton.

Two Little Angels

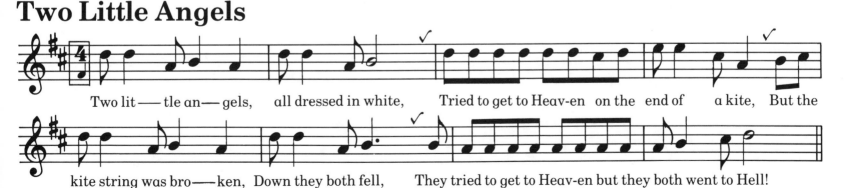

Two lit——tle an——gels, all dressed in white, Tried to get to Heav-en on the end of a kite, But the

kite string was bro——ken, Down they both fell, They tried to get to Heav-en but they both went to Hell!

New rhythms: See *Recorder from the Beginning* 2, pages 28–31 and 40–41.

Ye Banks and Braes (Scottish) Count ①–2–3–④–5 then play on count 6.

Let the Toast Pass (Scottish)

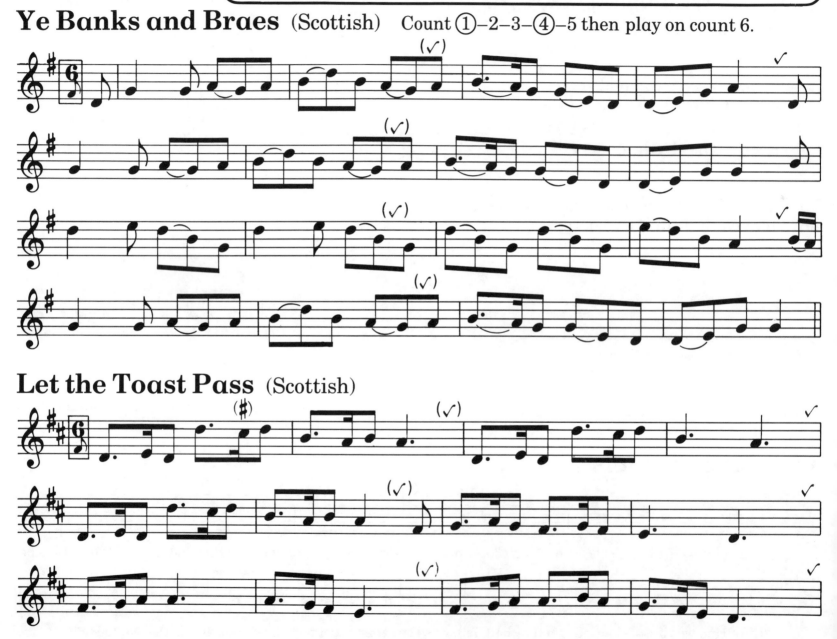

Ask a friend to play this rhythm on tambourine
as an accompaniment:

Glenlogie (Scottish)

When you can play **Glenlogie**
well, ask someone to accompany
you by playing this ostinato.
Use the largest (lowest-sounding)
xylophone you have.

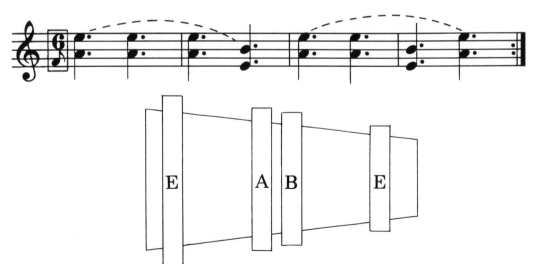

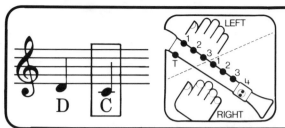

New note: lower C.
See *Recorder from the Beginning* 2, pages 36–37 and 42–45.

Annie Laurie (Scottish)   Count 1–2–3 then play on count 4.

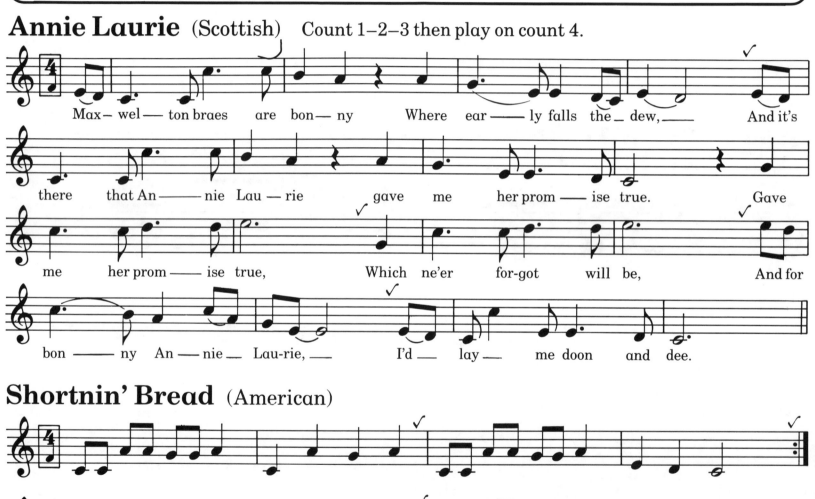

Max— wel—— ton braes   are bon— ny   Where ear —— ly falls the _ dew,——   And it's

there   that An———nie Lau—rie   gave   me   her prom——ise true.   Gave

me   her prom——ise true,   Which ne'er   for-got   will be,   And for

bon ——— ny An —nie_ Lau-rie, ——   I'd — lay — me doon   and dee.

Shortnin' Bread (American)

28

Morning Has Broken
(Gaelic)

This tune has nine crotchets in a bar in three groups of three. Count and conduct three slow beats per bar before you begin.

My Bonny Cuckoo (Irish)   Count ①–2–3–④–5 then play on count 6.

My bon—ny cuck-oo, ___ I tell you true, That through the groves I'll _ rove with you. I'll

rove with you un — til the next spring, And then my cuck-oo shall sweet ——ly sing. I'll

rove with you un — til the next spring, And then my cuck-oo shall sweet ——ly sing.

Ask some friends to accompany you. They can play any one or all of the ostinati below. It is best to use three different instruments.

rove with you. I'll

bon — ny cuck-oo, ___ my

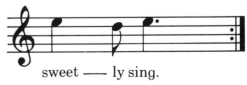

sweet —— ly sing.

Tune writing using notes we know

Try pages 46–47 in *Recorder from the Beginning* 2 before you start this page.

C D E F♯ G A B C′ C♯′ D′ E′

See if you can make up some music to finish off the tune on the next page. Follow the instructions carefully.

A Say and clap line 1, then play it.

B Make up the missing part of line 2. First play the beginning that is given. Then say and clap the words of the rest of the line up to "deep". Now make up a tune to fit the words you clapped.

Use any of the notes you know. Keep trying until you like your tune. Make sure it fits the rest of the tune. Then write it down.

C Say and clap line 3 then play it.

D Finish line 4 in the same way. Say and clap the words first. Keep trying different notes to fill the spaces until you like the tune. Then write down the notes.

Now play the whole tune.

Tired Caterpillar

A tired old cat—er—pil—lar went to sleep In a

hole in the for—est so snug and deep. And he

said, as he soft——ly curled in his nest,

"Craw—ling is plea—sant but rest is best!"

Fingering Chart
English (Baroque) Fingered Recorders

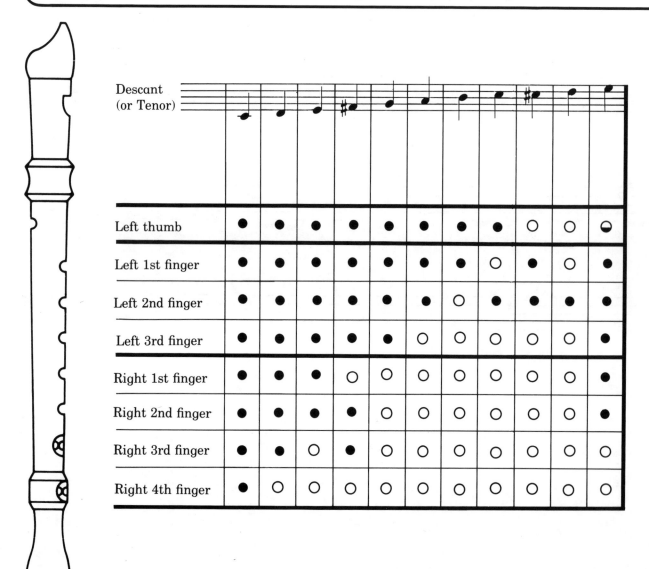

Descant (or Tenor)											
Left thumb	●	●	●	●	●	●	●	●	○	○	◑
Left 1st finger	●	●	●	●	●	●	●	○	●	○	●
Left 2nd finger	●	●	●	●	●	●	○	●	●	●	●
Left 3rd finger	●	●	●	●	●	○	○	○	○	○	●
Right 1st finger	●	●	●	○	○	○	○	○	○	○	●
Right 2nd finger	●	●	●	●	○	○	○	○	○	○	●
Right 3rd finger	●	●	○	●	○	○	○	○	○	○	○
Right 4th finger	●	○	○	○	○	○	○	○	○	○	○

○ Open hole
● Closed hole
◐ or ◑ Partly closed hole

10/01 (41590)